The Real Feelings

Poetry for every Heart

Kavita Kothari

Made with ❤ on the BookLeaf Publishing Platform
www.bookleafpub.in
www.bookleafpub.com

Dedication

This book is dedicated to complex feelings and all the
experiences humans feel and are hard to express

Preface

"Welcome to this collection of poems, where life's journey is woven into words. Within these pages, you'll find reflections on love, loss, hope, and resilience. May these poems be a mirror to your own experiences, and may they inspire you to cherish the beauty in everyday life."

Acknowledgements

I am thankful for the beautiful nature around us to heal and Inspire with every experience of life.

1. Far & Near

I always and again and again fall in love with someone
who is far but near,
Every part of my heart thinks of u
Though we are apart, we can't depart.

U r in my thoughts,in my dreams
U r my soul you are everywhere,
We are old school lovers,but everything
Between us always looks new & forever.

Don't ask me what I remember
A lot of things about us I can't get over....
Your tight hugs around my neck
You look angelic when u give me a peck...

Today if I could ask for anything it would be wings,
Would fly high and be in your arms with a swing,
Never a moment with u is dull
Waiting to enjoy every twist & twirl....

I want to see u fight,smile,cry,love and care,
All your emotions and affections are mine,
All my care and cuddles are yours.......
And so you are mine.....forever.......

Missing you Each day,
Makes me love you more and more......
Now I just can't wait to hug you
And give a kiss with love and adore......

2. Sometimes

Sometimes we talk
and it becomes a song
that dances in my veins
a melody of courage
i never knew was there

You met me
in the small corner
of this vast world
a beautiful accident
that turned my heart into gold

You are my cool shade
after the bright sun
Just want to express
that home is not a place,
But It's a feeling among us.

Our connection
is a language unspoken

each look, each laugh,
Is etched in our hearts
into something more

In silence, we converse
i see you, you see me,
I know in my darkest days
You are the light that keeps me shining and glee.

Sometimes when miles stretch
between us,
These are sometimes spent with you
Make me cry, make me Laugh
My heart knows the world is small
I blink my eyes, I will be home and that home is you.

3. The era of Barter

I wish time froze in old age
the birds never knew of their cage
where kindness flowed like rivers
and life felt harder but was easier

let's imagine a barter world
where hearts trade warmth for trust
I would give kindness and take affection
humbleness would earn me attention

On dark days when shadows loom
my heart would share warmth and love
in moments of stress and anxiety
I would find solace in empathy

Those days would bloom in gentle light
love wouldn't hold onto grudges

every exchange would spark connection
as we gave only love to each other

4. Waiting is good

The Wait

We always wait for
the next one to come
the days move slowly
while we wish for sun

when nights feel heavy
we long for soft light
the sky holds its breath
for clouds to bring rain

the soil whispers soft
cheering for raindrops
the sea dreams of rivers
with a gentle embrace

the temple bells chime
waiting for the prayer
waiting is an art

of hope and of time

I wait for the time between you and Me.

5. Hand in Hand - A hold

My hand in your hand makes me feel fearless,
It takes away all my stress.
I feel I am strong enough,
However the roads are tough.
Every time you hold my hand...
Higher I can fly ,
I am not afraid to touch the sky.
If I fall with your hand in my hand,
It feels smooth and gentle on the land.
Every time you hold my hand...
Holding your palms against mine,
Is a deep promise to make each other shine.
Hand in Hand we can walk miles together,
Alone in this world I would shatter.
Every time you hold my hand...
Our hands make the promise to raise & rise
As we are with each other in every sunset and sunrise.

6. Tattoo of my heart

Tattoos of my heart
engraved in my heart

Time spent with you
is a treasure
captured without lenses
moments and memories
siblings at heart
they tickle my soul
with every recollection

some chase wealth
others chase fame
I gather moments
woven with sentiments
that feels like home
when I am alone
they laugh, they cry
as the years take flight

I long for occasions
where sweetness awaits
to create true magic
ensuring your fragrance
never bids farewell
this bond we cherish
will always stay gold
Our story will never turn old.

7. Temporary truths

the gain and the pain don't stay
love and hate come and go
friends and enemies shift like seasons
roses bloom while thorns fade
breezes calm and storms disrupt
days and nights must find balance
you and me hold both our joys
let's choose happiness every time

8. Love Naturely

Your love to me is like a shade
Your presence is the aroma of the soil of first rain
Your arrival is a storm vanishing my anxiety and pain
Your company is like a sea-shore calm & composed
When you talk it feels it's raining all affirmations
When we laugh it feels like some telepathic connections
Our eyes talk with each other like birds chirp at the dusk
Our heart beats for each other like the sun shines at the
dawn.
I really feel we are made for each other,
like sky and sand faraway but always together...

9. The Walk

The Walk

Long walks with you are always serene,
I like when you hold my hand where the roads are lean.
On a walk with you the talks are real and silly.
There are no filters with you really
A long walk with you is a promise we share,
No matter what we will always care.
When your palms touch mine ,
I feel everything will be fine.
When we walk together our hearts pound fast
I want those moments forever to last.
Your heart beat is divine music,
When the feet are aligned it feels like real magic.
I want to walk with you forever,
And create a journey to remember.

10. If stars could see...

If the stars could glare,
They would see how much I care.
I want to hold you when you fall,
I want to see you rise, that's all.

The stars are seeing from above
My heart is filled with love
Your every victory is mine,
Your smile is the only thing that makes me shine.

The stars witness how much I adore you,
Without you my days are blue
I want you now, forever and always,
An Eternal feeling in my heart stays.

Under the sky,in the light of stars
You can heal my scars
If the stars could see
Together we make a perfect "We".

11. Tears beyond fears

"Tears Beyond Fears

Above my deepest fears, my tears shine bright
In happiness, they fall like diamonds in the night
They speak the words I fail to say
And express the emotions that sway

When heartache hits, tears roll down my face
Allowing me to confront the pain and find my place
On my pillow, I weep and let go
Sweeping away sorrows, making room for hope to grow

Tears may seem like water, but they're so much more
Pearls of emotion, filled with feelings I adore
Some bitter, some sweet, but all mine to own
Tears that fall, unfiltered, and make my heart feel home

When tears roll down and shine, I know I'm alive

Feeling every moment, with heart open and wide"

12. Love like the Bark & the Branch

A day in a life of a tree when all fruits find a new home,
The blooming and colourful flowers also seek for a new
garden and chrome.

The season of Autumn sheds the leaves
Roots and leaves are always in search of light
The Tree now looks dull at sight.
Amidst all this chaos, in the cycle of life
The bark and the branches always hold each other and
everyone ,
They wait for spring's embrace ,
They stand still for all bloom to come
Bark and branches are deeply rooted in love
Pessimistic and together for years
A dry Autumn or a lush spring
Together through darkness or in the sun They stand
together as one.

13. Mirror and its Diplomacy

Who says the Mirror doesn't lie,
Does it show everyday once I die

It makes me look content & tall
It never shows the pain of my fall.

Everyday it creates a scene to make you look beautiful
It never describes behind the scenes it's awful.

Mirror stands with some rooted old beauty definitions
Never it gives an ear to your explanations

The mirror shows your jaws,spots and flaws,
I wish it showed some people always have strong paws.

I always heard mirrors tell the truth
But as we grew learned it's a myth.

Mirror adds glaze and shine

On a bad day it doesn't spare me.

The emotions within are shaken and broken,
Mirror inspires you to rise again or else false you will be
proven.

Mirror is my soulmate it has it's own vision,
But everyday it inspires me to be my best version.

14. If you ever miss me

"If You Ever Miss Me

We parted ways, but my heart remains,
Longing for you, through life's joys and pains.
If you ever miss me, just come over,
I'll be waiting, with a heart that's still yours.

You were my everything, my guiding light,
Breathing without you is a endless night.
I know I may not mean the same to you,
But my love for you will forever shine true.

Memories of our past linger on,
Echoes of laughter, tears, and sweet moments gone.
Though time and space may separate us wide,
In dreams, our hearts will still reside.

I've learned to smile, to hide the pain,

But my heart still whispers your name.
If you ever miss me, just come over,
I'll be here, with a love and warmth forever.

15. Between us

I can't get over it if you don't talk to me,
I don't feel good if things are bad between you and me,
My day starts with meeting you,
Our bond is like glue.
My words and gestures are unfiltered,
Around you in this world I am least bothered.
I have always found love is an illusion and delusion,
Spending some time with you my friend,for me is the
best solution.
Heartbreak with a friend gives more pain,
It is a bond with no loss no gain
It's not good what I always feel,
I need you in my life to revert and to heal
Wherever we go, wherever we stay
A rainbow of memories is shining beyond the grey.

18.

16. Ingredients of life

Slow cooked emotions and moments are known as
relations
A beauty of relation lies in its imperfections

A more of spice and little sugar
Sometimes sour and many times bitter
All these mixes make life better.

Maybe some days won't taste good
But sometimes,
The best ingredients are found in the people you meet
and not the food.

Every time I see good things in any human
I immediately pick one without hesitation
The universe is a dining table with good virtues
Why do we keep holding on bad hues

Every season comes with a new appetite and new fruit
There is always a new beginning after the fight

So let's savor each moment, each smile, each tear,
And cherish the people who make life's journey clear.

In the end, it's not the food that we eat,
But the love and the connections that make life sweet."

17. Silent Heart

In the stillness, awkward silences are the most noisy
ones,
They speak louder by staying mum, as words eagerly
await
To break the silence, yet what if they create any
nuisance?
Silence in fights is like salt on wounds, hearts yearning
For the happy sounds that once filled the air.

Quarrels among the eyes depart the heart, leaving
A void that only true conversation can heal.
Silent hearts are fragile, but by speaking from the heart,
They can mend, and the words that follow silence can't
keep calm.

In the life full of hustle , comfort comes when a true
loved one

Holds your palm, it's a gentle reminder that you're not
alone.

18. Missed-Understanding

We don't see each other, no glances exchanged
We don't talk to each other, our voices estranged
We don't even smile, no warmth in sight
We don't message by chance, our contacts blocked in
night

Past experiences echo, "We aren't wrong"
Some bad circumstances lingered, and didn't move along
I didn't mean to hurt you, you didn't think to curb my
pain
We fell into the trap of mis-understandings, like summer
rain

Why are our hearts and souls being so unkind?
Let's solve what's misunderstood, and leave the hurt
behind
I'm sure we just missed listening, and that's why we

stray and pay,
Ending up with a "Missed-understanding", day by day.

19. My own Company

I like being alone at night
The stars shine bright, it's a peaceful sight
No noise, no stress, just calm and rest
I enjoy my own company, I'm at my best

In the quiet, I find my way
I learn to love myself, day by day
I'm happy with me, I'm free and light
I like being alone, it feels just right

The world outside fades away
I'm happy in my own way
I don't need others to make me smile
I'm happy with myself, all the while

20. Souls are Pure

Every soul is pure and bright.
A spark of goodness, shining light.
We're all born kind and true,
And our souls stay pure, forever new.

We may make mistakes, we may stumble and fall.
Our souls remain immortal and pure,
But obstacles in life are unsure.
They make you do wrong and evil.
Nobody is born bad, chaos in life makes you devil.

In those tough days,
Stay calm and try to pray.
End of the day, everything makes hay.
Good deeds done are never buried.
They grow into plants and are flourished.

21. Thank you Life

Life was tough, it knocked me down
I struggled to get up, to turn it around
I thought I'd never make it through
But hope kept shining, seeing me through

I tried to run, I lived in tears
Helping me face my deepest fears.
Every time I fell,
I saw loved ones waiting, smiling at me
Giving me strength to keep going, wild and free.

Life's a journey, with ups and downs
But I won't give up, I'll wear my crown
I'll hold on to hope, and never let go
And rise above, with a heart that glows.
My story is a long ride,
Every chapter gives me glory and pride.

www.ingramcontent.com/pod-product-compliance
Lightning Source LLC
LaVergne TN
LVHW010918200726
843509LV00013B/1983